Volcano Bubbles

by Anne Giulieri
photography by Sylvia Kreinberg

I'm going to make a *volcano*.
To make a volcano
you have to make a big hill.
You can make your big hill from:

paper and glue

playdough

sand

cardboard

3

After you have made your big hill, you can make a volcano!

To make your volcano, you need:

bicarbonate of soda

a spoon

vinegar

a jar

red food-colouring

washing-up liquid

a jug

You can find all of this at home.
Mum or Dad can help you.

To make your volcano,
sit the jar in the top of
the big hill.

Get the jug.

The vinegar goes into the jug like this.

The red food-colouring
goes into the jug like this.

The washing-up liquid
goes into the jug like this.

Tip the jug into the jar like this.

The soda goes into the jar like this.

bicarbonate
of soda

Look!

Can you see all the red *bubbles*?

The red bubbles come out of the volcano.
Down, down, down they all go!

It is fun to make
lots of red bubbles.

You can make your volcano
with green or yellow or blue bubbles.
Making a volcano is fun!

Picture Glossary

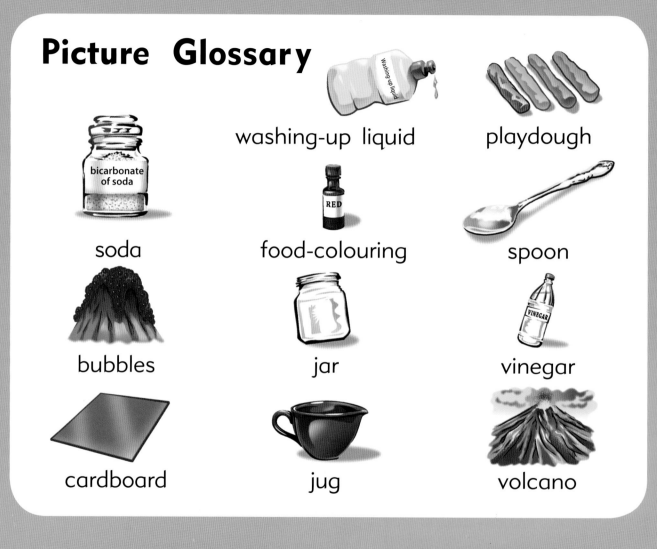

washing-up liquid

playdough

soda

food-colouring

spoon

bubbles

jar

vinegar

cardboard

jug

volcano